Drawings by

No Perfect People, Please!

poems created and read aloud by
Diane Asitimbay

Culturelink Press
San Diego, CA 92163

NO PERFECT PEOPLE, PLEASE!
Copyright ©2007 by Diane Asitimbay

All rights reserved. No part of this publication may be reproduced or transmitted in any form or by an means, electronic or mechanical, including photocopying, recording, or by an information storage and retrieval system, without written permission from the publisher, Culturelink Press, P.O. Box 3538, San Diego, CA 92163
Graphic Design by Kirsten Chandler

For ordering information, contact Culturelink Press at 619-501-9873.

Asitimbay, Diane.
   No perfect people, please! : poems / by Diane
Asitimbay ; drawings by Jim Whiting.
   p. cm.
   Includes CD of 11 poems read by the author.
   SUMMARY: Humorous poems that celebrate the unique
perspective of children.
   ISBN-13: 978-0-9759276-2-5
   ISBN-10: 0-9759276-2-0

   1. Children's poetry, American. 2. American poetry.
3. Humorous poetry.   I. Whiting, Jim (Jim V.), ill.
II. Title.

PS3601.S58N6 2007   811'.6
                     QBI07-600161

Printed in China

ABOUT THE CD
This audio CD includes:
- Approximately 10 minutes of engaging poetry on 11 tracks
- The Table of Contents shows the poems recorded and the track numbers
- Each poem shows you the track number on the page.
- Eleven poems read by the author, Diane Asitimbay

Visit our website: www.culturelinkpress.com

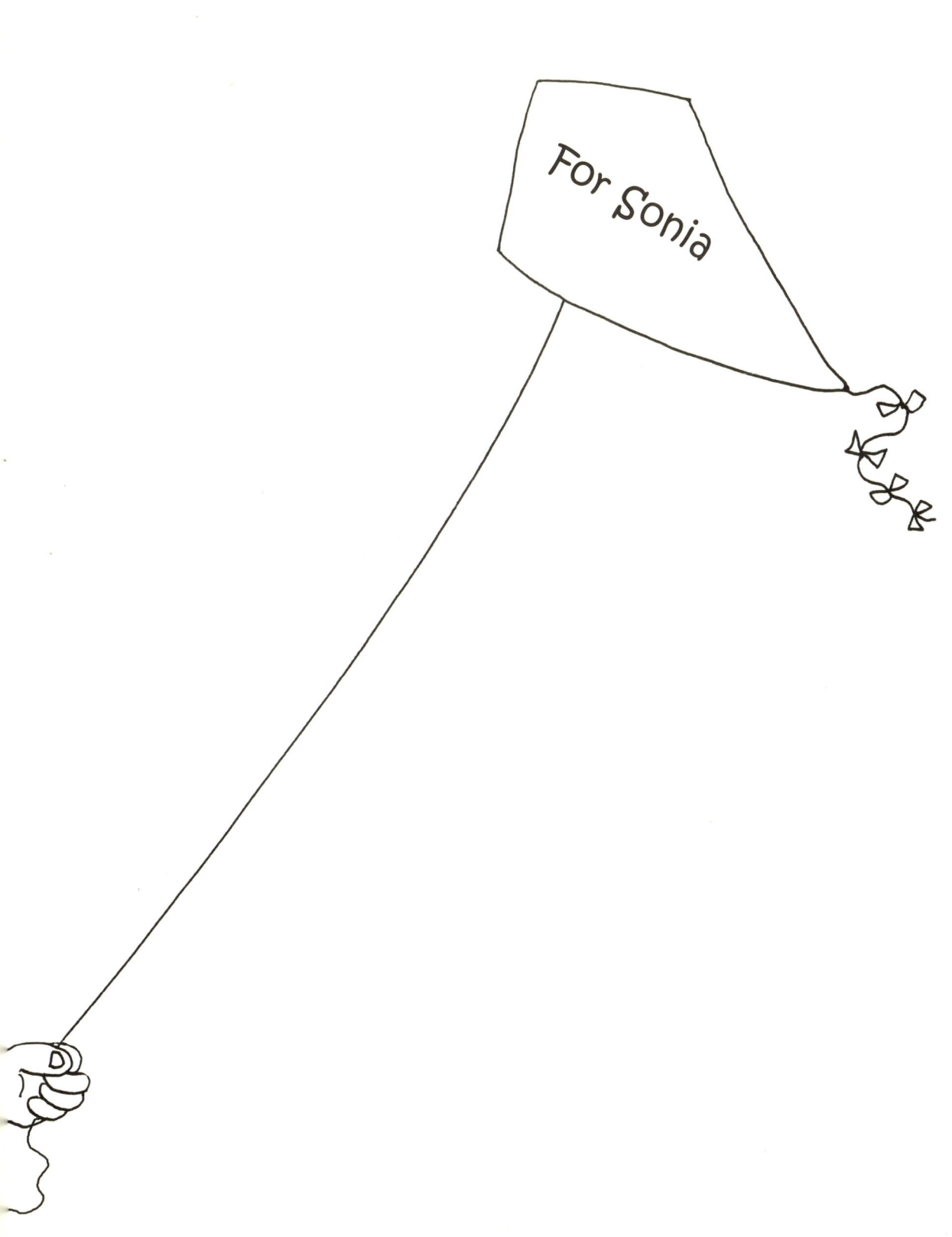

Contents

Page   CD Track

	Page	CD Track
Adam Amazola's Amazing Appetite	8	1
Brad Bradwurst the Braggart	10	
Colleen the Copycat	12	
Demanding Danny Duffet	14	2
Evan the Eavesdropper	16	
Funny Fernando Flores	18	
Grimy Gilbert Grantski	20	3
Hyper Harry Hildebrant	22	4
Irma with the Incredible Imagination	24	
Jealous Jeanie Johnson	26	
Klutzy Kyle Kilgory	28	
Lazy Larry Leopold	30	5
Mini Millie Miller	32	

	Page	CD Track
Nosy Nellie Nelbert	34	
Ordinary Omar Orton	36	
Picky Peter Pindell	38	6
Quiet Quimby Quigley	40	
Rude Ruth Rukby	42	7
Shy Sheila Shelly	44	8
Tyler the Tattle Teller	46	9
Upset Ursula Uggerman	48	
Vain Victoria Vite	50	
Whiny Willie Whipple	52	10
X-ray the Extreme Expert	54	
Yolanda the Yacker	56	11
Zippy Zelda Zimmerman	58	

Adam Amazola's Amazing Appetite

Adam Amazola is always hungry.

His mother says
he's growing like a weed,
for he's impossible to feed!

It's like he has a hole in his shoe,
and there's no way to fill him up
no matter what you do!

So while Adam's tummy is growling,
his mother is howling,
for the food bill is out of sight,
due to Adam's amazing appetite.

"He eats me out of house and home,"
his mother will say,
as she packs his lunch each day.
She tries to fill his belly
with peanut butter and jelly.

Wherever Adam is,
he's hunting for something to eat.
It can be salty or it can be sweet,
and when there's no food around,
Adam bites his nails to calm himself down.

Adam Amazola
has outgrown his sleeves,
three sizes, would you believe!

His pants are too short, his mother reports.
"My, oh my," his mother cries,
"He's only ten,
and he needs new clothes again?"

Taller and taller, Adam grows.
How tall he'll be,
no one knows.

Brad Bradwurst the Braggart

Brad Bradwurst is the biggest braggart
on the planet.
He brags about a billion times a day,
in a bratty, braggaty way.

He brags about being
the best baseball player on the block.
He brags about his big brother,
who plays hard rock.

Brad the braggart
has the biggest head
you ever did see.
It's swollen up real big,
like he has an allergy.

And then one day,
it happened so fast,
when Brad the braggart
got a B in class,
and everyone else
got an A that day,
and do you believe
the braggart didn't know what to say?

So when Brad the braggart ran out of luck,
his bragging got stuck.
His head shrank to normal size,
and to our surprise,
not a bratty thing did he say,
and all his bragging went away.

Colleen the Copycat

Colleen is a Copycat
Imagine that!
Anything you do,
she will copy you!

If you get new tennis shoes,
Colleen the Copycat
will get some too!

If you join a dance class,
she'll sign up fast!

If you go to Disneyland,
she'll say she went there too,
even when Colleen the Copycat
knows it's not true!

Colleen the Copycat!
What can you do?
She's something like
a twin you grew!

It's like looking in the mirror and saying
Boo! or Shoo!
Instead of seeing only one of you,
You always see two!

Demanding Danny Duffet

Demanding Danny Duffet
never waits
for what he wants.

A choo-choo train, a moo-moo cow,
a dog that goes bow wow,
Danny wants it NOW!

Uh-oh!
he sees a truck, what luck!
Here it comes!
The beat of his drum –
Tum tee tum tum
It's time
for Danny to throw his tantrum.

Demanding Danny Duffet
drops to the floor
of the department store.

He kicks and cries,
while watching his mother's eyes,
twisting and turning and squirming,
he screams and screams,
until people stop and stare,
and glare from everywhere.

He howls and growls,
until his mother gives in,
and Danny wins,
She buys him the toy, oh boy!

Uh-oh!
Now Danny Duffet sees a backpack!
Get ready for the next act!
Here comes another,
just like the other.
Listen to the beat of his drum,
tum tee tum tum
Danny's TANTRUM.

Evan the Eavesdropper

Evan is in his heaven
when one enormous ear
stretches to the front,
and the other to the rear,
and he pretends not to hear
the grown-up gossip that's near.

But it just so happens,
he'll overhear
the most exciting events first.
And when he does,
he'll burst!
He'll run to tell someone right away,
what others whisper that day.

I heard it!
I heard it first!
I heard it very clear!
For you see,
I have this most enormous ear.

You should have heard!
You should have heard
what they said about
him and her and you.

You wouldn't believe it,
but I heard it,
so it must be true,
what they said about
him and her and you.

I have the news,
all the news you can use!
Yes I do!
All the news,
that can fit in one ear.

For I heard it first,
and I heard it clear,
when it blew into
my enormous ear.

Funny Fernando Flores

Fernando Flores is truly funny.
He's so funny
that your nose gets runny.
When he tells you a joke,
you nearly choke.

Fernando is so outrageous
his giggle is contagious.
Your gut gets stuck
in a chuckle-chuck.

You bite your lips,
you hold your hips,
you need some grips
for the giggle trips.

Your belly aches,
your jaw shakes,
your ribs feel sore,
and you can't take it anymore.

You moan and groan.
Your guts are about to pop!
So you tell Fernando to
"PLEASE STOP!"

"I need to catch my breath!
Or else I'll laugh myself to death!"

Grimy Gilbert Grantski

Grimy Gilbert Grantski
doesn't mind
any kind
of grease or grime.
"A speck of dirt never hurt,"
he would say.

Now Gilbert won't rub.
And he won't scrub.
And he plays with the water in the bathtub.
And over time,
his grease and grime
have turned to slime.

He won't wash his hair,
And white things, like snowflakes,
fall from his hair,
and land on his chair.
But Gilbert just tells his friends
"I don't care!"

Gilbert won't let his neck get wet.
He says, "What the heck!"
So if you check his neck today,
it's a mucky yucky gray.

He won't soap up his feet.
Needless to say,
they smell not so sweet!

Gilbert's ears are filled with wax
and in the backs, they're totally black.
A good Q-tip he lacks.

Not a tooth will Gilbert brush,
He plays with the paste until it's mush,
and then dribbles water on his toothbrush.

So that's why at night,
when Gilbert turns off the light,
his teeth are kind of yellow,
when they really should be white.

Hyper Harry Hildebrant

Hyper Harry Hildebrant
has ants in his pants,
and sitting still
makes Harry squeal.

It's true! It's true!
Teachers carry glue
to stick Harry's bottom to the seat,
and paste the floor to Harry's feet.
But Harry can't sit still for long,
before he needs to run around.

He's up, he's down,
he's up again, oh no!
He's up and down
like a yo-yo.

He bats a ball, whacks a wall,
races you and chases you,
hangs a hoop, lets out a whoop,
kicks a can, and shows you a handstand.

For Hyper Harry Hildebrant
has ants in his pants,
and sitting still
makes Harry squeal.

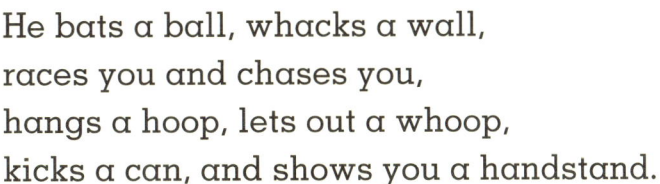

Irma with the Incredible Imagination

You can't always see
what Irma sees.
You see plain old trees,
but Irma sees
jungle creatures
that knock your knees.

You eat a simple banana,
and it tastes like a banana.
But when Irma takes a bite,
the banana turns into a tropical delight,
for Irma pictures a far-off land,
where monkeys screech to get a tan.

You see, Irma makes up stories
about places that could be,
which are even better than
the commercials on TV.
With just her imagination,
Irma goes anywhere
she wants to be.

And the food Irma dreams of
is so incredible
it's not edible.

Like peanut-butter spiders,
cockroach sliders,
and strawberry-filled worms that make you squirm.

Irma is so creative
that we secretly believe
she has a magic bone
hidden in her sleeve.

Jealous Jeanie Johnson

Jealous Jeanie Johnson
likes to play with one friend, not two,
for three makes her jealous, you see.

Jeanie Johnson
wants a friend
that's all her own,
for she doesn't want
to play alone.

She has no trouble with a double,
but Jeanie turns meaner
when there's an in-betweener.

Her teachers and mother discuss
the true meaning of "us,"
and how nice Jeanie needs to be,
whether there are two,
or whether there are three.

No matter what she's told,
even after the scold,
Jeanie wishes for a you and me—

Oh, how happy she would be,
if there were just two
and not three!

Klutzy Kyle Kilgory

Klutzy Kyle Kilgory
is klutzy
no matter whatsy.

    He falls over
    sidewalk bumps,
    garbage lumps,
    and tree stumps.

        Two broken toes,
        a bloody nose.
        Poor Kyle, that's how it goes.

            He trips over
            newspaper racks,
            grocery sacks,
            and sidewalk cracks.

His knees get bruised,
and out of whack,
and Kyle nearly breaks his back.

    He crashes into
    closed doors,
    open drawers,
    and slips on waxy floors.

        Kyle nearly splits his spine,
        and gets a very sore behind.

            Who drives you nuts
            with all his cuts?
            Why it's Kyle Kilgory
            the King of Klutz!

Lazy Larry Leopold

Lazy Larry Leopold
is no fool.
He lies in his bed every morning
until he's late for school.

Then out of bed
he'll creep,
to look for
another place to sleep.

You can find him in the back row
of the classroom,
where he snoozes,
in the corner he chooses.

You can find him
secretly nodding off
in the corner
of the choir loft.

What are we to do?
For Lazy Larry
snores at movies too!

Sometimes he sleeps so deep
he looks like a loaf of bread.
You begin to wonder
is he alive, or is he dead?

No, Larry isn't crazy.
He's just plain old lazy.
It's useless to scold.
He's simply Larry Leopold!

Mini Millie Miller

Mini Millie Miller
is so skinny,
the food she eats is
hardly any.

"Eat 15 pies!"
her mother cries.
So Mini Millie
tries and tries
to eat 15 pies,
and then some meat.

She even tries to eat
fried duck's feet.

But all in vain,
for not a bit of fat
does she gain.

Mini just stays thin.
Skinny she is,
and skinny she's been,
and skinny she'll be,
till who knows when.

Nosy Nellie Nelbert

Nosy Nellie Nelbert
looks you in the eye,
and asks you sweetly,
Why?
Who is that guy?
What's that?
Where's your cat?
How come?
Why can't I have some?

And for some weird reason,
you need to reply,
and even when you try,
you cannot lie!

Today, she asks you,
"What's the matter?"
And it's like you turn nuts.
Before you know it,
you spill your guts!

"What's wrong?" you ask.
"Well, today,
my head is shot,
my throat is hot,
there's a hair in my eye
and a splinter in my thigh."

"I have corns on my toes,
a pimple where my earring goes,
a pain in my chest,
and what question is next?"

And when you're done telling
Nosy Nellie Nelbert
everything there is to know,
more and more
Nosy Nellie wants to know.

For Nosy Nellie
is really a pro
at finding out all the details,
before she lets you go.

Ordinary Omar Orton

There are lots of things you can be,
and one of them is just ordinary.

Omar Orton is just ordinary.

Nothing odd or unusual
about him.
He wears a medium
in pants,
and an average in a shirt.
Being ordinary doesn't really hurt.

Omar is just a normal kid
who gets C's in school,
not A's or B's.
He's not a genius.
but he's not a fool.

Omar likes to be a part of a crowd,
not stand out, and not be loud.
He isn't quiet, and he isn't wild.
He's a pretty easy child.

You can always count on Omar
between drama kings and other extremes.
For there are lots of things you can be,
and one of them is ordinary.

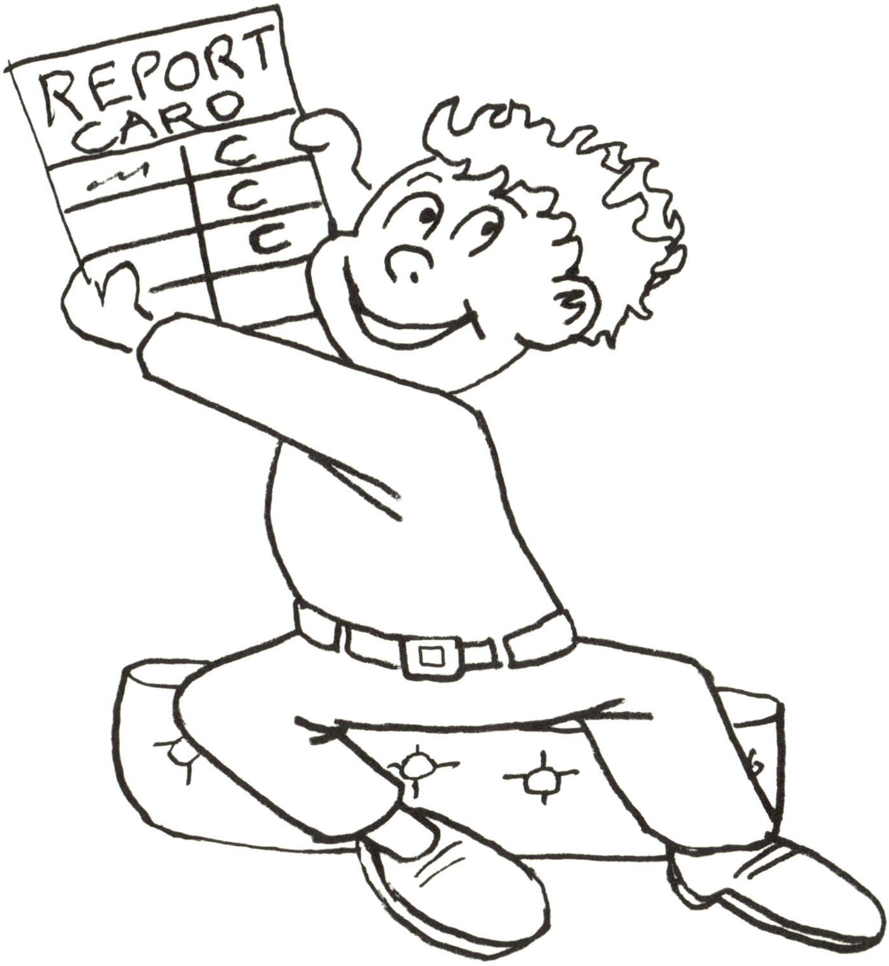
REPORT
CARD
C
C
C

Picky Peter Pindell

Picky Peter Pindell
is very picky.
If something isn't right,
he calls it icky.

At dinner,
Picky Peter's seat
must be the perfect height.
And the onions in his meat
must be completely out of sight,
before he takes an itty bitty bite.

Picky Peter Pindell
is very picky,
so going to bed
can be a bit tricky.
In order for Peter to go to sleep,
his bed must be very, very neat.

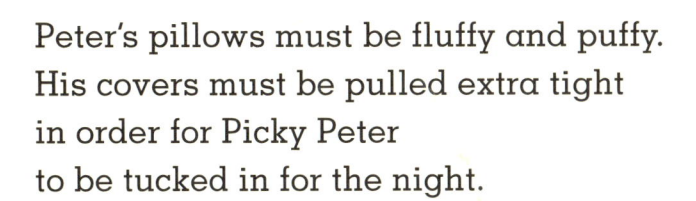

Peter's pillows must be fluffy and puffy.
His covers must be pulled extra tight
in order for Picky Peter
to be tucked in for the night.

Picky Peter Pindell
is so picky
that everything Peter Pindell picks,
his poor mother hurries to fix.

Quiet Quimby Quigley

Quiet Quimby Quigley
never chews a stick of gum,
but he has a secret habit.
He sucks his thumb!

His mother is so worried
she dips his thumb
in hot sauce, curried.
But Quiet Quimby
sneaks a suck.
He covers his mouth
like his finger is stuck.

Mrs. Quigley,
in order to cope,
writes to the Pope.
While waiting for his most holy advice,
she puts Quimby's thumb on ice.

His thumb turns numb,
but his bad habit has stayed,
so Mrs. Quigley wraps his thumb in a thick Band-Aid!
Which makes the taste of the thumb delayed.

But Quiet Quimby Quigley
sneaks a suck.
He covers his mouth
like his finger is stuck.

Then Mrs. Quigley buys him
a stuffed bear to hug.
And, after that,
a fuzzy wuzzy blanket to lug.

But Quiet Quimby Quigley
sneaks a suck,
under the covers,
like his finger is stuck.

Now Mrs.Quigley has tried everything!
She's losing hope on getting help from the Pope,
so Mrs. Quigley starts sucking *her* thumb
and joins Quimby in his comfortdom.

Rude Ruth Rukby

Ruth Rukby
is rude and crude,
and has this
incredibly bad attitude.

She likes to watch people gasp and run,
when she makes a face,
and sticks out her tongue.

And when you talk to her,
she looks away,
and she interrupts you to say,
"Dude!" and "No way!"

She rolls her eyes and lets out sighs.
   In your face, she flips her hair,
     and says "Who cares?"

     Ruth's table manners are worse.
       She licks her fingers, and she burps.
      When she chews her food,
     she opens her mouth
    for us to see,
   what she's chewing so noisily.

  Because Rude Ruth
   loves to stun and shock
   all the polite kids on the block,
 I'm sorry to tell you the sad truth, but
nobody really likes Rude Ruth.

Shy Sheila Shelly

Ask her
what her name is,
and shy Sheila
shivers and quivers.

Ask her again,
and she looks around,
and stares at the ground.
"Sheila," she whispers,
"and I'm shy."

"Speak up, Sheila!"
her teachers all say.
"I will," she answers,
"but not today."

Then on parent-teacher conference day,
Shy Sheila Shelly's mother appears.
A very loud and large woman.
A mother everyone fears.

Shy Sheila's mother shouts,
"HOW'S MY LITTLE GIRL?"
"IS SHEILA BEHAVING?"
"Yes," the teachers all say.
"But we're afraid Sheila is so shy,
she seldom has anything to say."

Now Shy Sheila's mother
looks so troubled and perplexed,
she doesn't know what to say next.

Finally she screams,
"HOW COULD THIS BE?"
"MY SHEILA TAKES AFTER ME!"

When Shy Sheila's mother says goodbye,
her teachers finally understand why
Shy Sheila Shelly is so shy.

Tyler the Tattle Teller

Tyler the Tattle Teller
rat a tat tat!
Tattles on this,
And tattles on that.

A tall tattle
a small tattle,
from a teen to a tot,
Tyler the Tattle Teller
tattles a lot.

He tattles on Kate,
and she's only two.
He tattles on Nate,
a grown up, it's true!

rat a tat tat
rat a tat tat
Tyler keeps tattling
while his teeth are rattling,
until one day,
his teeth all rot away.

One by one,
Tyler's teeth
wiggle and jiggle
and then fall out,
right in the middle of his tattling route.

Then Tyler picks up all his tattley teeth,
and tucks them under his pillow one night,
so the Tooth Fairy will find them,
in his envelope sealed tight.

Well, the Tooth Fairy came,
and saw his rotten teeth.
Not a cent did she leave!
Not a single penny did
Tyler the Tattle Teller receive.

Upset Ursula Uggerman

Ursula Uggerman
is mysteriously upset.

One minute Ursula Uggerman
is your best friend
to the end,
and the next minute,
she won't talk to you.
What did you do?
You have no clue!

Ursula grins,
but then she frowns.
Her smile
suddenly
turns upside down!

Ursula goes
from happy to sad,
glad to mad,
at least 25 times a day.
That's just
the upset Ursula way.

No one knows
which mood
Ursula is currently in,
or when another mood
might begin.
But every day,
we can surely bet,
Ursula will get
mysteriously upset.

Vain Victoria Vite

Vain Victoria Vite
thinks she's always right.
And since she thinks
she's very bright,
she likes to pick a fight.

Because she's teacher's pet,
in case you forget
her trait of being great,
she'll set you straight.
If you're not exactly right
she'll get uptight.

She'll correct you
until you're right,
So if you change your mind,
which you might,
you could end up in a nasty fight.

But if you're completely mistaken,
you might be shaken,
for she'll chew you to bits
and spit out the pits.

You'll lose your wits,
until you admit
the mistake you did commit.
For Victoria Vite
thinks she's always right.

Whiny Willy Wipple

Whiny Willie Wipple
whines,
not double,
but triple.

Willy whines about
his homework to do,
drags his backpack,
and asks,
"Oh, do I have to?"

"We're going to have dinner,"
announces his mother.
*"Can you get out the bowls
for your favorite stew?"*
Willie whines,
"Oh, do I have to?"

Willie whines about
cleaning up his dog's doo doo, pee yoo!
"Oh, do I have to?"

Nothing makes you more weary
Than listening to Willie clearly
whining all day long,
with the same old song,
"Oh, do I have to?"

X-ray the Extreme Expert

X-ray
is a computer expert,
and he's the best that you can find,
when you have a computer problem
of the very frustrating kind.

Do not be embarrassed
that he is only nine.
Remember, you have a deadline!

Now after you've tried and tried,
to find your computer bugs inside,
just swallow your pride,
and call X-ray today,
because your solution is only
a phone call away.

You need X-ray to know
what makes your computer so slow.
He'll calm your worst fear,
if your files disappear.

When you're stuck with uploads and downloads,
X-ray will save the day.
For any software
he can add or take away.

Since X-ray fixes your computer for free,
everyone is his friend,
or at least tries to be!

So call X-ray today,
And tell him you'll pay
with a burger and fries,
but you better hurry,
before your computer dies!

Yolanda the Yacker

Yolanda the Yacker
talks too much.

Yackety-yack
Yackety-yack.
What she yacks about
no one can keep track.

She yacks so much
that it's a fact,
a knack for silence
she does lack.

A "hm um …"
"Is that so?"
"Really?"
You need not say,
for Yolanda to continue
on her yackety-yack way.

She yacks in your face,
she yacks to your back,
she yacks about this,
and she yacks about that.

Yolanda yacks so much
that, in fact,
you have no chance
to yackety-yack back.

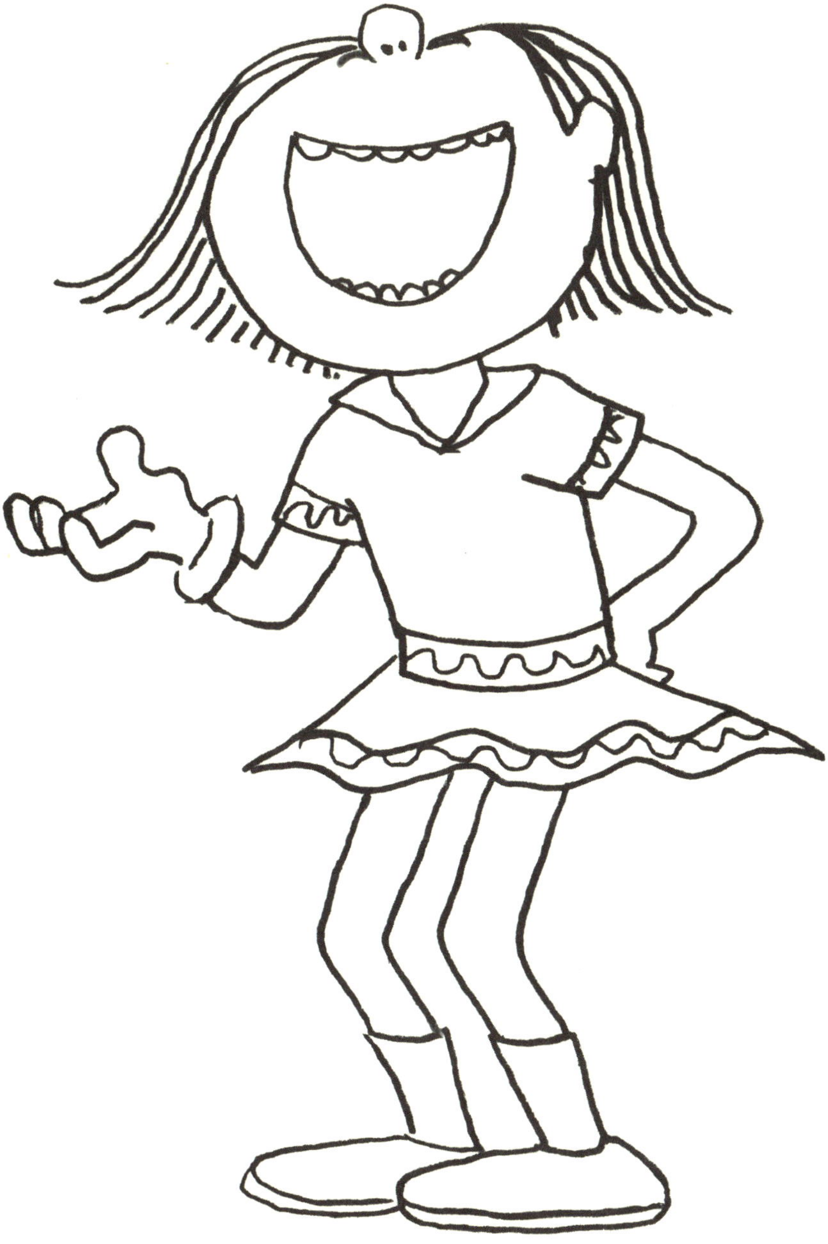

Zippy Zelda Zimmerman

Zippy Zelda Zimmerman
zooms by
like a hungry fly,
sniffing a pie,
a zippety zip
in a lickety-split.

Zippy Zelda Zimmerman
dips and tips
on her scooter
named Tooter,
like a slippery snake
who ate
a chocolate cake.

Zippy Zelda Zimmerman
flies and flees
past you and me,
like a stressed bee
on a shopping spree.

Zippy Zelda Zimmerman
hurries and scurries
like a mouse who worries
about the cheese she sees.

Zelda has so much zippety zip
You want to run with her,
jump and skip,
a zippety zip,
in a lickety-split.

But just when you want to say, "Hi!"
Zippy Zelda is on her goodbye!

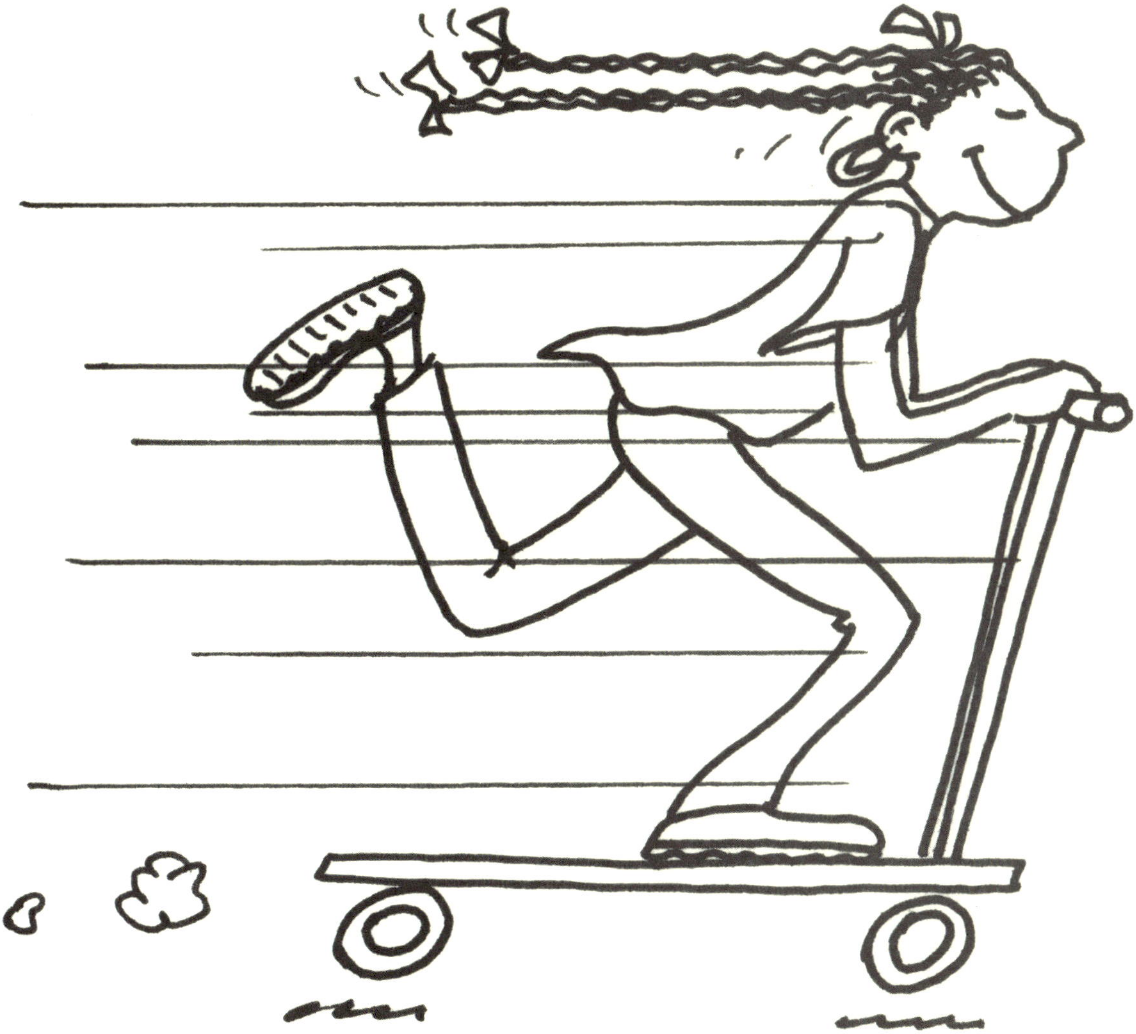

First Line Index

Adam Amazola is always hungry.
Brad Bradwurst is the biggest braggart on the planet.
Colleen is a Copycat
Demanding Danny Duffet never waits for what he wants
Evan is in his heaven when one enormous ear stretches
Fernando Flores is truly funny.
Grimy Gilbert Grantski doesn't mind any kind of grease
Hyper Harry Hildebrant has ants in his pants
You can't always see what Irma sees.
Jealous Jeanie Johnson likes to play with one friend
Kyle Kilgory is klutzy no matter whatsy.
Lazy Larry Leopold is no fool.
Mini Millie Miller is so skinny

Nosy Nellie Nelbert looks you in the eye
There are lots of things you can be
Picky Peter Pindell is very picky.
Quiet Quimby Quigley never chews a stick of gum
Ruth Rukby is rude and crude
Ask her what her name is, and shy Sheila shivers
Tyler the Tattle Teller rat a tat tat!
Ursula Uggerman is mysteriously upset.
Vain Victoria Vite thinks she's always right.
Whiny Willie Wipple whines, not double, but triple.
X-ray is a computer expert
Yolanda the Yacker talks too much.
Zippy Zelda Zimmerman zooms by

My thanks
to my husband Angel and my daughter Sonia,
for all the times they looked and listened,
and looked and listened some more to me
while I was writing this book.

For the wonderful insight and editorial guidance,
I'd like to thank Lindy Ferguson and Walter Kleine.

I'm very grateful to have worked with
such talented artists as Jim Whiting and
graphic designer Kirsten Chandler.

A big THANK YOU to all of you!

Diane

~ The End ~